Chocolate Paste Cakes

ADRIAN WESTROPE & DAN TABOR

MEREHURST

Dedication

I would like to dedicate this book to my Mom and Dad for their unending support throughout the years. I would also like to give special thanks to Jenny and Duncan for putting up with me (and the chocolate) for three months. Dan

I too would like to thank my Mum and Dad for their tremendous help over the last year. I wish to dedicate the book to all my friends all over the world. Adrian

First published 1996 by Merehurst Limited
Ferry House, 51–57 Lacy Road, Putney,
London SW15 1PR

Copyright © Merehurst Limited 1996
ISBN 1-85391-579-3

A catalogue record for this book is available from the British Library.

Editor: Helen Southall
Design: Anita Ruddell
Photography by Clive Streeter

Colour separation by Bright Arts, Hong Kong
Printed in Hong Kong by Wing King Tong

Contents

INTRODUCTION 4

Techniques 4
Basic Recipes 7

Introduction

A new and exciting cake decorating medium with an irresistible flavour, chocolate paste can be used in much the same way as sugarpaste.

For many people, modelling chocolate will be a new cake decorating medium. The increasing popularity of using chocolate to decorate cakes makes it possible not only to coat a cake with chocolate, but also to finish it with chocolate decorations.

We are all chocolate lovers at heart but up until now it has been impracticable for most to attempt coating a celebration cake with chocolate, other than using the pouring method. This book introduces those who use sugarpaste (rolled fondant) to a delicious alternative. Not everyone enjoys the taste of sugarpaste, and modelling chocolate is an exciting substitute.

All of the projects in this book are completely edible, no wires or other inedible items having been used in their making. By using white, milk and dark chocolate, you can create almost any colour, thus extending the range of design possibilities. For example, it can be a problem designing a suitable

celebration cake for a man, but with chocolate paste you can utilize the colour aspect of chocolate, enabling you to accomplish this with ease, as illustrated by some of the projects in this book – see the Fruit Barrel (page 44) and the Cuckoo Clock (page 30).

Chocolate paste can be used on fruit, madeira and chocolate sponge cakes, as well as on gâteaux, tea fancies and torten. It is suitable for covering, modelling and moulding.

Techniques

Rolling chocolate paste

With this medium, it is not possible to roll directly on a work surface; you must always roll chocolate paste between plastic sheets. During colder months, it is advisable to warm the paste gently in a microwave oven for 20–30 seconds on medium before you start to roll it. If you haven't got a microwave, warm the oven to about 160°C (325°F/Gas 3), then turn it off. Put the chocolate paste in a heatproof dish, cover it and put it in the oven for 4–6 minutes until warmed.

Knead the chocolate paste until it is pliable, flatten it

slightly, and then place it on a sheet of plastic. (Use good quality plastic, e.g. a large freezer bag. Avoid using thin plastic, such as cling film (plastic wrap), as this will crease when rolling.) Cover the paste with another plastic sheet and roll with a rolling pin until the desired thickness is achieved. Remove the top sheet of plastic, then replace it and turn the paste over. Repeat to release the underside. If the paste clings to the plastic, gently rub your hand over the surface of the plastic to warm the paste slightly. Any embossed pattern, such as basketweave or ribbing, should be added at this stage.

Making cut-out shapes and mouldings

There are occasions when you need to use plain set chocolate or mouldings. To do this, melt the chocolate in a bain-marie (double boiler or a heatproof bowl over a saucepan of simmering water), and either pour it into chocolate moulds or spread it thinly on a board covered with non-stick paper. When set, you can cut out the desired shapes using either a sharp knife or cutters.

Above: Equipment for use with chocolate and chocolate paste
Below: A selection of decorative chocolate moulds

Painting with chocolate

Using a small amount of melted white chocolate mixed with edible petal dusts (blossom tints), you can paint on to the surface of chocolate paste. Additional painting can be achieved using petal creams (see page 6).

Making chocolate /sugarpaste mix

By mixing equal quantities of chocolate paste (see page 7) and sugarpaste together, you can make a paste that retains the flavour of the chocolate but is a more elastic paste suitable for covering any height and shape of cake. Gently knead the two together, trying not to incorporate too much air. To roll the mix, no plastic sheet is necessary, but it might be advisable to dust the rolling surface with icing (confectioners') sugar.

Covering cakes

Chocolate/sugarpaste mix

When using chocolate/sugarpaste mix (see above), it is possible to cover a whole cake by the 'all-in-one' method.

1 Brush the cake with apricot glaze or mask with buttercream. Roll out the paste mix large enough to cover the top and sides of the cake.

2 Lift the paste on the rolling pin and drape it over the cake. Starting at the top, smooth out any folds or pleats, gradually working down the sides. Use a sugarpaste smoother for a good finish.

3 Trim off the excess paste at the base of the cake.

Chocolate paste

The all-in-one method can also be used to cover shallow cakes with chocolate paste. For high-sided cakes, cover the top and sides separately.

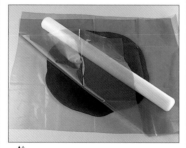

1 Roll out the chocolate paste and release it from the plastic as described on page 4.

2 Cut out a piece of paste to fit the top of the cake. For a square cake, cut panels of chocolate paste and position them around the cake sides. For a round cake, cut a strip of paste to fit the circumference of the cake.

Colouring chocolate paste

For an overall base colour, add a little paste or liquid food colouring to the glucose mixture when making chocolate paste (see page 7). To enhance coloured paste, additional colouring can be kneaded into the paste prior to using. Use the tip of a cocktail stick (toothpick) to add the colour in tiny amounts, kneading the paste after each addition, until you achieve the required colour.

Chocolate paste can also be tinted after shaping with petal cream, which can be purchased in a wide range of colours in small tubs. If you cannot obtain them, you can make your own by adding a small amount of petal dust (blossom tint) to melted cocoa butter (available from health food shops and specialist suppliers, see page 48). You can either paint the cream on with a brush or rub it on with your fingers.

Piping chocolate

Add glycerine to melted chocolate (1 teaspoon to 125g/4oz chocolate), stirring it in until the mixture thickens slightly. Use a greaseproof paper piping bag fitted with a suitable tube (tip). If the mixture becomes too stiff, place the bowl in the microwave for a few seconds on medium, or warm over hot water.

Basic Recipes
Chocolate paste

Milk, dark or white chocolate can be used in this recipe. The better the quality of the chocolate (the higher the cocoa butter content), the better the results (and the flavour) will be. Oil flavourings, such as orange, lemon, peppermint, etc., can be added to the glucose mixture to either enhance or change the flavour completely.

500g/1lb chocolate
150g (5oz) liquid glucose
50g (2oz) liquid sugar
(see right)

1 Break up and melt the chocolate in a bain-marie (double boiler or heatproof bowl over a saucepan of simmering water), but do not overheat.

2 Combine the glucose and liquid sugar in a bowl, warm and add to the chocolate.

3 Stir the mixture with a wooden spoon until blended, but do not beat. Transfer to a plastic bag and store for 24 hours at room temperature before using. Do not place in the refrigerator. (If paste is kept too cool, condensation will form on the surface and a bloom will develop.) To store for longer (up to 3 months), double wrap in plastic and place in an airtight container in a cool, dry place.

4 Before using, knead the paste until pliable. Larger amounts should be warmed (see page 4).

Liquid sugar

Mix together 4 parts granulated sugar and 3 parts water in a saucepan. Bring to a rolling boil, and boil for 3 minutes. Cool to room temperature and store in a glass container with a tightly fitting lid. Keep cool but not refrigerated.

Gum glue

60ml (2fl oz/¼ cup) tepid water
¼ teaspoon CMC
(gum tragacanth substitute)
or gum tragacanth

Put the water in a bowl, sprinkle in the gum, and whisk vigorously. Pour into a screw-top jar and allow to stand for several hours. Store in the refrigerator.

Christmas Cake

For this unusual Christmas design, the cake is covered with green and white chocolate paste and finished in a very traditional way with a candle and holly.

Materials

200g (6½oz) white chocolate paste
25x20cm (10x8 inch) long octagonal fruit cake covered with marzipan (almond paste)
Vodka
345g (11oz) pale green chocolate paste
Gum glue
60g (2oz) dark green chocolate paste
60g (2oz) marzipan (almond paste)
60g (2oz) red chocolate paste
60g (2oz) chocolate chips
½ teaspoon glycerine
60g (2oz) yellow chocolate paste
Melted chocolate for assembly

Equipment

Thin card
Plastic sheets
30x25cm (12x10 inch) long octagonal board covered with dark green foil
Ribbed rolling pin
Border lace cutter
Clay gun with discs, optional
Large and small holly leaf cutters
Dresden tool
No. 56 (101)petal piping tube (tip)

Preparation

1 Cut a card template of the top of the cake using the cake tin as a guide.

2 Roll out the white chocolate paste and use the template to cut out a long octagonal shape to fit the top of the cake. Stick to the surface with a little vodka. Place the cake on the board.

3 Roll out the pale green paste and pattern with a ribbed rolling pin. Cut a strip the depth of the cake and long enough to wrap around the sides. Attach to the cake with a little vodka, making sure that the join is neat. Trim to fit.

Base and top borders

4 Roll out a strip of white paste, pattern with the ribbed rolling pin, and cut out a lace edge with the border lace cutter. Carefully paint a line of gum glue around the cake base and attach the patterned strip, trimming to fit.

5 Take a small amount of dark green paste and, using the clay gun fitted with a ribbon

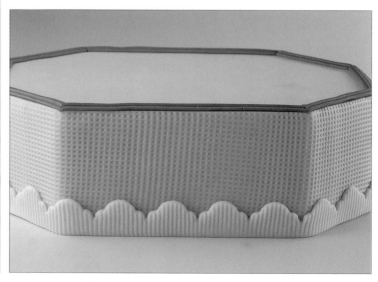

disc, squeeze out a strip. Cut and fit strips to form a border around the top edge of the cake, sticking with gum glue. (Cut strips by hand if you haven't got a clay gun.)

Top decorations

6 Roll the marzipan into a thick sausage shape. Using thinly rolled red chocolate paste, cover the marzipan, cutting to fit. Taper one end and add grooves in bands with the edge of a palette knife. Model a tiny wick from white paste, and add to the tapered end.

7 Roll out some dark green paste and cut out a selection of holly leaves. Vein with a dresden tool, and place to one side. Roll a selection of tiny red balls for the holly berries.

8 To make fir cones, melt the chocolate chips and thicken with the glycerine (see page 7). Place in a small piping bag fitted with a no. 56 (101) petal tube. Using piping bag cones for bases, pipe out a selection of different-sized fir cones. Allow to set. Remove by gently twisting off the paper.

9 Use the clay gun fitted with a rope disc to create a twisted rope (or make by hand). Attach tassels, made by hand or using the clay gun fitted with a hair disc.

10 Place the candle on the top of the cake, slightly off centre, sticking with melted chocolate. Start to add the large holly leaves with a little gum glue. Add the fir cones, fixing with melted chocolate. Place the smaller holly leaves at the base of the cake. Add the rope and holly berries to the top and more berries to the cake sides.

Victorian Lace Wedding Cake

This 3-tier cake is decorated with full lace sections to match the cake base colour, and completed with cranberry and cream coloured roses. All items on this cake are made out of a chocolate/sugarpaste mixture and the cake is therefore entirely edible.

Materials

15cm (6 inch), 20cm (8 inch) and 25cm (10 inch) square fruit cakes covered with marzipan (almond paste)
1.75kg (3½lb) white sugarpaste (rolled fondant)
1.75kg (3½lb) white chocolate paste
Vodka
Icing (confectioners') sugar for dusting
Gum glue
Green and red petal creams
Green and cranberry paste food colours

Equipment

Sugarpaste smoother
23cm (9 inch), 28cm (11 inch) and 36cm (14 inch) square cake boards covered with cranberry coloured foil
Clay gun with discs, optional
Silicone lace mould
8 cake pillars
Plastic sheets
Small and medium rose leaf cutters

Preparation

1 After covering the fruit cakes with marzipan, allow to stand for 48 hours.

2 Combine the sugarpaste and chocolate paste to make a chocolate/sugarpaste mix (see page 5).

3 Brush the marzipan on each cake with a little vodka. Roll out the chocolate/sugarpaste mix, using a little icing sugar to dust the rolling surface. Apply to the cakes using the all-in-one method of covering (see page 6). Place the cakes on their boards.

Base border and lace

4 Using a clay gun, make a thin twisted rope and attach with gum glue to the base of each cake. (If you haven't got a clay gun, make ropes by hand.)

5 For the lace, roll out some chocolate paste mix 2.5mm (⅛ inch) thick, and lay it

over the negative side of the mould, gently pressing the paste into the mould. Place the positive side of the mould on top and press. Remove the paste section from the mould and trim to the size required as necessary. Each cake requires 12 lace pieces (but see Note on page 12).

6 With gum glue, paint the underside of each piece of lace and attach around the sides and on the corners of each cake. Position eight lace pieces to create the base layer, then attach another piece on top at the corners of each cake, creating a tiered effect.

7 Roll out some more paste and cut out four extra sections of lace for the top of each cake (for the flowers to be placed on). Stand the pillars in place on the top surface of the bottom two cakes, to help with the positioning of the flowers and leaves.

Roses and buds

8 ▷ Start with a cone of chocolate/sugarpaste mix and set aside. Cut eight pieces of paste and roll into balls, each the size of a marble. Cut one more piece that is twice as large as the others to form the bud petal. The size of the cone and balls of paste will determine the size of the finished rose.

9 ▷ Place the balls of paste between plastic sheets and thin half of each using your thumb or finger. It is important to leave the base of each petal thick. Remove the top sheet of plastic and peel off the 'bud' petal. For the cream-coloured roses, tint the edge of the petal slightly by gently rubbing with a small amount of red petal cream.

10 ▷ Place the cone a quarter of the way in from the left-hand edge of the petal and 2.5mm (⅛ inch) down from the top edge. Wrap the left-hand half of the petal around the cone to the front, making sure that the bud forms a sharp point at the top. Wrap the larger right-hand half round to the front, curling the edge of the petal back when you have completely enclosed the cone.

11 ▷ For a bud, roll the base between your fingers and cut off the excess paste. For a full rose, release another petal from the plastic, tint the edge as before and place on the bud, covering the curled back edge of the first petal, and cupping around the bud. Add two more petals to completely encircle the bud. Each petal should overlap the previous one by 5mm (¼ inch). The bud and petals should be at the same height.

12 ▷ Attach another five petals, curling their edges back slightly and tinting to give the rose an open look. Leave to dry for a few minutes, then roll the base of the rose between

your fingers and cut off the excess paste.

Leaves

13 ▷ Colour 60g (2oz) chocolate/sugarpaste mix pale green. Roll out and cut a selection of rose leaves. Thin the edges, vein and pinch into shape with your fingers. Leave to dry. With a small amount of red petal cream on your fingers, wipe the set leaves to shade the edges.

Assembly

14 ▷ Arrange the roses, buds and leaves in the centre of each cake, on top of the lace pieces, attaching with a little melted chocolate if necessary. Some simple green buds can be used to fill out the arrangement.

Note

The number of lace pieces needed will vary according to the size of cake, and the size of the lace mould you are using. Hold your mould up against each cake to work out how many pieces you will need, and whether you will need to trim them to fit.

12

Child's Truck

This novel cake can be decorated in many different ways. The large side panels could carry inscriptions or painted characters.

Materials

25cm (10 inch) square madeira cake, 7.5cm (3 inches) high
Jam and buttercream
220g (7oz) white chocolate paste
220g (7oz) white sugarpaste (rolled fondant)
Selection of paste colours and petal dusts (blossom tints)
90g (3oz) black chocolate paste
Gum glue
15g (½oz) cocoa butter
Melted chocolate for assembly
30g (1oz) dark chocolate paste

Equipment

Large, sharp, serrated knife
Round cutter
Sugarpaste smoother
45x18cm (18x7 inch) oblong board covered with blue foil
Dresden tool
Herb cutter, optional

Shaping

1 Using a large, serrated knife, cut two strips of cake, one 10cm (4 inches) wide and the other 5cm (2 inches) wide. Slice both strips horizontally and sandwich with jam and buttercream. Cut the 5cm (2 inch) strip in half and place side by side on top of the 10cm (4 inch) strip.

2 Make the cab with the remaining cake by cutting the strip in half to create two 13cm (5 inch) pieces. Sandwich the two pieces together with buttercream, and trim to shape the cab.

3 Use a round cutter and a craft knife to cut out one wheel arch on each side of the cab. Repeat this for the trailer, cutting out four on either side.

Covering

4 Combine the white chocolate paste with the sugarpaste to make a chocolate/sugarpaste mix (see page 5). Reserve 30g (1oz) white and colour 250g (8oz) cream. Reserve 45g (1½oz)cream paste and roll half of the rest to an oblong 2.5mm (⅛ inch) thick. Mask one side of the trailer with buttercream and place this side on to the rolled paste. Trim to fit, leaving an extra 5mm (¼ inch) at the wheel arches.

5 Turn the trailer the right way up and, using your fingers, gently work the paste into the wheel arches. Smooth the side and trim where necessary. Repeat to cover the opposite side of the trailer.

6 To cover the front, top and back of the trailer, colour 155g (5oz) chocolate/sugarpaste mix rust, and roll out a wide strip 45x10cm (18x4 inches) and approximately 2.5mm (⅛ inch) thick. Trim the strip to the exact width of the trailer. Mask the front, top and back with buttercream and place the paste strip over the entire length. Using a smoother, flatten the surfaces and trim off the ends.

7 Cover the cab in a similar way, but place the long strip over the cab first, and then apply the side panels.

Features

8 Using 60g (2oz) black chocolate paste, model 10 wheels to fit inside the wheel arches, and model an exhaust pipe and bumper. Out of leftover pieces of paste, colour and model a selection of lights for the cab and trailer, and a wind deflector for the top of the cab, and set aside.

9 Colour some paste a darker rust, and cut and mould a grill for the front of the cab. Roll and cut a thin strip of white paste mix, glue and attach to form the windows. Cut a thin

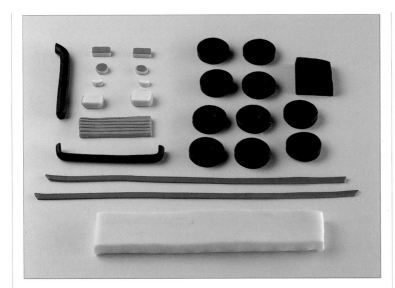

strip from each end of the front window, and replace with a strip of rust paste to create the door frames.

Finishing

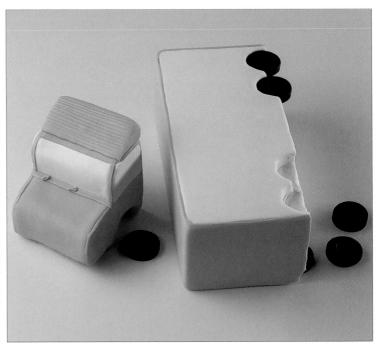

10 With a selection of petal dusts and warmed cocoa butter, paint the sides of the trailer with your design or inscription. Paint wipers on the windscreen.

11 Turn the trailer on its side and attach the wheels with a small amount of melted chocolate. Using the 45g (1½oz) reserved cream paste, roll out a thick narrow strip and attach with buttercream to the bottom of the trailer between the wheels, keeping the height the same as the wheels. Turn the trailer upright and attach to the board with melted chocolate.

12 Position the wheels on the cab. From 30g (1oz) black chocolate paste, cut two small squares, 5mm (¼ inch) thick, and attach one to the back of the cab with melted chocolate to create the connection for the trailer, and place the other underneath the cab to elevate slightly.

13 Position and glue the exhaust pipe on the back of the cab. Attach the cab to the board in front of the trailer with melted chocolate. Use a dresden tool to mark lines for the cab doors.

14 Attach all the previously made pieces to the cab, i.e. headlights, grill, bumper, etc., with gum glue. Position and glue the lights to the rear of the trailer. Roll the dark chocolate paste to an oblong 2.5mm (⅛ inch) thick. Use a herb cutter to cut thin strips, or cut very thin strips with a sharp knife, and attach to the trailer edges with gum glue, trimming to fit.

Horse Head

The popularity of horses should make this cake a favourite
with young and old alike.

Materials

30cm (12 inch) square madeira
cake
Buttercream and jam
360g (11½oz) dark chocolate
paste
345g (11oz) sugarpaste (rolled
fondant)
45g (1½oz) white chocolate paste
Gum glue
30g (1oz) black chocolate paste
7g (¼oz) cocoa butter, melted
Edible gold petal dust (blossom
tint)
Melted chocolate for assembly
15g (½oz) red chocolate paste

Equipment

Thin card
Sharp serrated knife
36cm (14 inch) square cake
board covered with gold foil
Bone tool
Small round cutter
Herb cutter, optional
Pasta machine with spaghetti
rollers, optional

Shaping

1 Using the photograph on
page 19 as a guide, sketch
a rough outline of a horse's head
on to thin card, and cut out.

2 Using the template, carve
the horse's head from the

cake with a sharp serrated
knife, and place on the work surface. Trim off sharp corners, and
hollow out a round hole for the
nostril and a pointed oval for the
eye. Cut a slit for the mouth.

3 From a scrap of cake, cut
a shallow dome to pad out
the jaw. Attach with jam. Mask
the head with buttercream.

4 Combine 345g (11oz) of
the dark chocolate paste
with the sugarpaste to make a
chocolate/sugarpaste mix (see
page 5).

5 Accentuate the eye and
nostril by rolling small
sausages of chocolate/sug-
arpaste mix and placing them
around these areas.

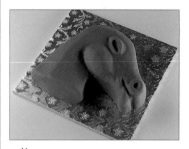

6 Roll out 625g (1¼lb) dark
chocolate/sugarpaste mix,
and use to cover the horse's
head by the all-in-one method
(see page 6), trimming to fit.
Place the cake on the board.
Using a bone tool, gently push
the paste into the nostril, eye
socket and mouth areas. Roll out
and cut a strip of white chocolate paste and position along the
horse's nose, rubbing the edges
to blend in.

Features

7 For the eye, shape a wal-
nut-sized piece of white
chocolate paste to a pointed oval
to fit inside the socket. Make the
pupil by rolling a pea-sized piece
of dark chocolate paste very

thinly and cutting out a small round disc. Attach to the eye with gum glue and position inside the eye socket.

8 With 30g (1oz) chocolate/ sugarpaste mix, model two ears by cutting the paste in half and rolling each into a ball. Form into a cone and flatten. Use your finger to hollow out the inside of each ear and pinch to refine the edges.

9 Mould a ring, about 2.5cm (1 inch) in diameter, from a pea-sized piece of dark chocolate paste, and set aside.

10 Form the reins and bridle straps by rolling out the black chocolate paste to 2.5mm (⅛ inch) thick, and cutting long strips 5mm (¼ inch) wide. Score with a dresden tool. Place the ring at the edge of the horse's mouth and attach the straps to the head with gum glue, looping them through the ring. Trim to fit.

11 Model a 'bit' by rolling a pea-sized piece of dark chocolate paste into a sausage and inserting it into the mouth, looping it over the ring. Paint the bit using melted cocoa butter mixed with a small amount of edible gold petal dust.

12 Attach the ears to the forehead using a small amount of melted chocolate, holding them in place until the chocolate has set.

Brow band and mane

13 Roll separately 15g (½oz) white chocolate paste and 15g (½oz) red chocolate paste to 2.5mm (⅛ inch) thick. Cut into strips using a herb cutter or sharp knife. Weave the strips together and trim to two strips wide and 13cm (5 inches) long. Position on the forehead and attach with gum glue.

14 Roll 60g (2oz) dark chocolate/sugarpaste mix through a pasta machine set at number 4. Pass through the 'spaghetti' roller, and cut to 10cm (4 inches). (Alternatively, push paste through a sieve, or roll fine strands by hand.) Attach in sections from the back of the neck, draping to the front. Continue to attach the mane until you reach the ears, allowing a few strands to drape on to the forehead.

15 With gum glue, attach the rein, looping it through the ring and laying it over the mane at the base of the neck.

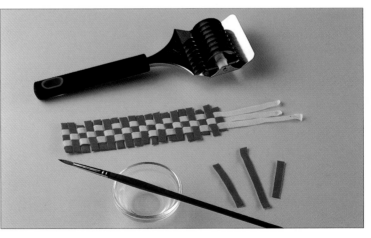

Sewing Basket

This project illustrates the versatility of both white and dark chocolate paste. The many coloured pieces used are all made from white chocolate paste, and make a good contrast against the dark basket.

Materials

875g (1¾lb) dark chocolate paste
Gum glue
200g (6½oz) white chocolate paste
25cm (10 inch) long octagonal chocolate cake
Chocolate buttercream
Melted chocolate for assembly
315g (10oz) chocolate paste of various colours
Vodka
Black paste food colour

Equipment

Thin and thick card
Plastic sheets
Basketweave rolling pin
Foam pad
Tapered grooved cone tool
Dresden or veining tool

36cm (14 inch) long octagonal cake board covered with silver/grey foil
Sugarpaste smoother
Clay gun with discs, optional
Piping bag
Cocktail sticks (toothpicks)
Smocking pin
Silicone moulds
Anglaise cutters

Lid

1 Cut a thin card template of the top of the cake, using the cake tin as a guide. Repeat using thick card to make a lid. Cut this in half. Roll out a piece of dark chocolate paste large enough to cover both halves of the lid. Roll over once with the basketweave rolling pin, and cut the paste in half, following the line of the weave.

2 Paint the thick card with gum glue. Invert the paste on to a piece of plastic so the basketweave is face down, and place both halves of the lid, glue-side down, on the paste, with the long edge of each half lid aligned with the cut edge of

the paste. This will ensure that the basketweave pattern will be straight and even on the lid. Separate the halves by cutting through the paste.

3 Press gently on the backs of the lid pieces to secure the paste to the board. Carefully turn one half on to your hand and peel off the plastic. Cut off the excess paste. Repeat for the other half of the lid.

4 Turn the lid pieces over on to a piece of foam so the basketweave is down. Brush a small amount of gum glue on the centre of each lid.

5 Roll out a piece of white paste, making the edges fairly thin and leaving the centre quite thick. Cut this piece of paste in half and place one half on each side of the lid, with the thick area at the long edge of each half. This paste should not cover the entire lid; leave a 2.5cm (1 inch) border all around the edge. Paint this with glue.

6 Roll out a very thin piece of white paste large enough to cover both halves of the lid completely. Cut this in

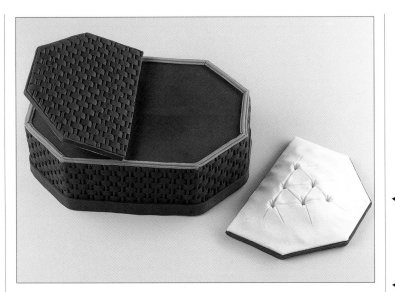

ger up and down the seam to blend the two ends together. Press a smoother against the sides of the cake to adhere the paste and create a smooth surface.

Borders

11 Roll out a long, thin strip of dark paste and cut to 1cm (½ inch) wide. Attach this strip around the base of the cake. Trim the ends evenly.

12 Make a decorative edge for the top by pushing paste through a clay gun fitted with a flat strip disc, or cutting fine strips by hand. Secure with gum glue.

Attaching the lid

13 Roll two tapered sausages of paste, glue and place one either side of the centre of the cake. These will be used to prop the lid at an angle.

14 Pipe melted chocolate down the centre of the cake and position both halves of the lid. Make sure the cushion on each half is resting on the sausage of paste. (It may be necessary to use cocktail sticks/toothpicks to hold the lid pieces in position until the chocolate has set.)

Contents

15 Mould a selection of different-sized buttons

half and place one half over the 'cushion' on each lid piece. Press to seal, and trim around the edges.

7 Push a tapered, grooved cone tool into the thick parts of the 'cushion', and accentuate the cushion effect by drawing lines from one indentation to the next using a dresden or veining tool. Roll a thin strip of dark paste, and cut it to fit the thickness of the lid. Glue the strip on to finish the edges of both lid pieces.

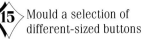

Covering the cake

8 Cut, layer and mask the cake with buttercream. Roll out a thin piece of dark paste and, using the template, cut out a long octagonal shape to fit the top of the cake. Place on top of the cake and trim off excess paste. Place the cake on the board.

9 Roll out a strip of paste long enough to wrap all the way around the cake, and as wide as the depth of the cake. Roll over once with the basket-weave rolling pin. Using the weave as a guideline, cut a strip to the height of the cake, and peel away the excess.

10 Carefully pick up the strip of paste and, starting at a corner, wrap it around the cake, making sure not to indent the paste with your fingers. Trim the ends to meet perfectly. Gently run your fin-

from coloured paste. Model cotton reels by hand. To make 'thread', roll out a piece of coloured paste, and roll over it once with a smocking pin. Trim to fit the width of the cotton reel, and wrap the thread around the reel.

16 Make a selection of textured material pieces out of coloured pastes, e.g. broderie anglaise, leather strips, lace sections, chequered material, etc. Gather some of these pieces and allow them to set.

17 Make skeins of thread by hand or using a clay gun fitted with the hair or grass disc, loop around and gather at one end.

18 Cut a tape measure by rolling a thin strip of white paste and cutting to 1cm (½ inch) wide. Paint on the numbers and markings with black food colour mixed with a small amount of vodka. Make a 'cameo' by pushing paste into a silicone mould, and attach to a piece of paste material with gum glue.

19 Other items to be hand moulded could include a crochet needle, buckle, toggles, needle and pin cushion. All items need to be placed on either side of the basket under the lid and spilling out at each end. The basket should appear full. Place a few items on the board around the cake.

Finishing

20 Use a clay gun fitted with a rope disc to create a large twisted rope (or make the rope by hand). Glue and place down the centre of the basket where the two halves of the lid meet. Allow the rope to hang down slightly in the front and attach a tassel, made by pushing paste through a sieve, or using the clay gun fitted with a hair disc. Make and attach two smaller tassels to the ends of the lid, and finish with two small paste buttons.

Old Leather Book

This simple but effective design was inspired by an old-fashioned, leather-bound book with a very ornate cover.

Materials

28x20cm (11x8 inch) madeira cake layered with jam
Buttercream
155g (5oz) white chocolate paste
500g (1lb) dark chocolate paste
Piping gel

Equipment

Sharp serrated knife
33x25cm (13x10 inch) cake board covered with bronze foil
Large plastic sheets
Narrow ribbed rolling pin
Ruler
Dresden tool
Silicone moulds

Shaping

1 > Trim the long sides of the cake with a serrated knife to form a book shape. The spine edge should be slightly convex, and the pages concave. Mask the top and sides with buttercream, and place on the board.

Covering

2 > Roll a thin strip of white chocolate paste the length of the three page edges and as wide as the depth of the book. Roll over once with a narrow ribbed rolling pin and cut to the depth of the cake. Gently wrap this strip from spine base to spine top, trimming to fit.

3 > Roll out a small piece of dark chocolate paste and cut three strips 5mm (¼ inch) wide. Attach these strips around the base of the cake, cutting to fit. These represent the back cover of the book.

4 > Roll out more dark chocolate paste and cut out a rectangle 5mm (¼ inch) larger than the book in length, and as wide as the book plus the spine. Gently place the paste on top of the cake to form the top cover, and wrap around to create the spine, trimming to fit.

Decoration

5 > Using a ruler and a dresden tool, score some lines around the spine. Score

more lines just inside the top edges of the cake.

6 > Using silicone moulds, make a selection of shapes to embellish the book cover. Mould a crown.

7 > Cut a shield using a card template (see page 47) and place in the centre of the book cover. Score the edge with the dresden tool to define the shape. Attach scroll mouldings to the cover with piping gel. Attach the crown to the shield and finish with extra scrolls.

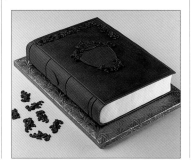
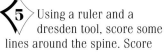

Friendly Dragon

This brightly coloured dragon is ideal for a child's birthday celebration.

Materials

30cm (12 inch) round cake
Buttercream
440g (14oz) white chocolate paste
440g (14oz) white sugarpaste (rolled fondant)
Green, cream and purple paste food colours
7g (¼oz) cocoa butter, melted
Black petal dust (blossom tint)
Gum glue
15g (½oz) black chocolate paste
15g (½oz) red chocolate paste
185g (6oz) desiccated (shredded) coconut
Green liquid food colour
280g (9oz) green royal icing

Equipment

Sharp serrated knife
Bone tool
Dresden tool
Round cutters
Plastic sheets
36cm (14 inch) square cake board

Shaping

1 Cut the cake vertically in half to form two half circles. Stand one half on the work surface on its cut edge to create the dragon's curved body.

2 From the remaining cake, cut and shape a head, elongating the nose and rounding off the top and sides of the head. Cut indentations for the nostrils and a slit for the mouth. From a scrap of cake, cut a small cube to form the neck, trimming to fit the body. Also from scrap cake, cut a shallow dome shape to pad out the leg area. Attach with buttercream.

3 Use buttercream to attach the neck piece to the body and to mask the surface of both body and head.

Covering

4 Combine the white chocolate paste with the white sugarpaste to make a chocolate/sugarpaste mix (see page 5). Colour 750g (1½lb) light green with paste food colour.

5 Accentuate the facial features by placing a thin sausage of light green mix around the top of the eyes and around the nostrils. Roll out 470g (15oz) of the green paste mix and use to cover the body by the all-in-one method (see page 6).

6 Roll out 60g (2oz) of the green paste mix, and use to cover the head. Cut the paste around the nose and remove. Use a bone tool to shape the paste gently around the eyes to accentuate.

7 Colour 30g (1oz) of the white chocolate/sugarpaste mix cream. Roll out and use to cover the nose. Carefully ease the paste into the nostrils with the bone tool, and define the mouth with a dresden tool. Gently rub your finger over the seams to blend.

Features

8 Mark fine grooves around the nose and eyes with the dresden tool. Use the melted cocoa butter mixed with a small amount of black petal dust to paint a line around each nostril.

9 For the eyes, roll out a small piece of the leftover

cream paste mix and cut two discs to fit the eye sockets. Attach with gum glue. Trim the bottoms of these circles straight with a sharp knife. Roll the black chocolate paste very thinly and cut out two 'pupils' using a small round cutter. Attach to the cream discs with gum glue.

10 Model ears from two small balls of light green paste mix. Form each ball into a cone and flatten slightly. Hollow out the centre of each ear with the bone tool, and pinch at the base to curve in. Cut off flat at the base and attach to the head with gum glue.

11 Make a tongue by rolling out the red chocolate paste very thinly. Cut a

4cm (1½ inch) strip 5mm (¼ inch) wide. Cut 1.5cm (¾ inch) of this strip in half and taper the ends to a point, curling up slightly. Set aside.

12 For the purple spots, colour 30g (1oz) of the white chocolate/sugarpaste mix purple. Roll out very thinly and cut out discs using a large round

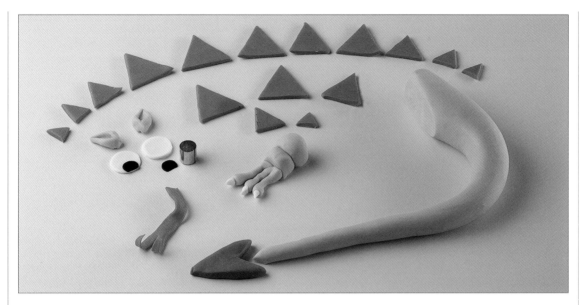

cutter. Stick these 'spots' on the body and head with gum glue, and gently rub the edges with your finger to blend with the green paste.

Tail

13 Roll 155g (5oz) light green paste mix into a ball and taper to form a cone. Continue rolling and elongating until the cone has reached a length of 18cm (7 inches). Trim the wide end of the cone flat and position at the rear of the body, curving the tail around to the front. Attach with gum glue. Use your finger to blend the end of the tail into the body.

14 Colour 60g (2oz) of the remaining white choco-late/sugarpaste mix dark green and use 15g (½oz) to mould a thick arrowhead shape. Attach to the end of the tail with a little gum glue.

Foot

15 Use 15g (½oz) light green paste mix and roll one third into a thin sausage. Cut into three equal pieces to create the toes. Roll each tube between your fingers to round off the ends. Place together with a small amount of gum glue, joining at the cut ends.

16 Cut the remaining two thirds of paste in half and roll into balls. Stick the two balls together, one behind the other, then position the toes just under the front ball.

17 Make toe nails by rolling three tiny balls of cream paste mix into cones, and attaching to the toes.

Board

18 Colour the coconut green by shaking it in a plastic bag with green liquid food colour. Using 250g (8oz) green royal icing, spread a thin layer on the board. Stipple the icing by lightly tapping the surface with the end of a dry pastry brush, creating small peaks. Generously spread the coconut over the wet icing, and tap off the excess.

19 Transfer the dragon body to the board with a large offset palette knife, then attach the head to the neck with a small amount of royal icing. Position the foot in front of the leg and attach with gum glue. Attach the tongue to the mouth.

20 Roll out 30g (1oz) dark green paste mix to 2.5mm (⅛ inch) thick and cut out approximately 18 varying-sized triangles. Attach small triangles to the head and tail, and the larger triangles to the body with gum glue.

Cuckoo Clock

With little or no added colour you can create a very realistic finished piece suitable for any occasion. This clock could make an unusual retirement, New Year's or even a groom's cake.

Materials

20cm (8 inch) square chocolate cake
Jam and buttercream
345g (11oz) white chocolate paste
500g (1lb) dark chocolate paste
30g (1oz) white chocolate chips
60g (2oz) dark chocolate chips, melted, for assembly
Bronze petal dust (blossom tint)

Equipment

Acetate sheet for templates
Sharp serrated knife
Plastic sheets
Dresden tool
Ruler
Set of round cutters
Piping bag
Silicone paper or cellophane
Thin card
Corn husk
Large leaf cutter
Foam pad
Ball tool
Small sharp scissors
45x30cm (18x12 inch) cake board covered with cranberry-coloured foil
Small closed scalloped crimper

Shaping cake

1 Make a template of the clock shape from acetate sheet, tapering the roof slightly and using the cake tin as a guide. Place over the cake and, with a sharp serrated knife, cut the shape from the cake. Layer with jam and mask the entire surface with buttercream.

Covering

2 Reserve 30g (1oz) of the white paste. Knead the remaining white paste into the dark to form a lighter colour.

3 Roll the chocolate paste to a thickness of 2.5mm (⅛ inch). Cut strips to the length and height of each cake side, including the peaked roof, and position these on the cake.

4 Using the template, cut another piece of paste to fit the top. Once this has been attached and trimmed, use a dresden tool and a ruler to mark a diamond pattern in the paste. Cut two more pieces for the roof of the clock, making them 2.5cm (1 inch) longer to create the eaves.

Clock face

5 Using a round cutter, remove a disc of paste from slightly below the centre of the clock. Cut through the paste and peel away the disc, then remove the cutter. Alternatively, make a template from the clock face on page 47, and cut the paste with a knife.

6 Knead the reserved 30g (1oz) white paste with 30g (1oz) of the dark paste to make an even paler colour. Roll it out and, using the same round cutter or template, cut out the clock face. Use smaller cutters to mark rings on the clock face.

7 Melt the white chocolate chips and add warm water, a drop at a time, stirring after each addition, to thicken slightly. Spoon into a piping bag and use to pipe Roman

numerals on the clock face (see page 47). Place the disc into the front of the clock. Using round cutters, cut out a ring of chocolate paste to fit around the clock face. Attach with gum glue.

8 Pipe the hands (see page 46) on silicone paper or cellophane, and leave to dry.

Remove from the paper and attach to the clock face with a small amount of melted white chocolate.

Front framework

9 Cover a large board with a piece of plastic for placing all items on to set.

10 To make a card template of the front framework, use the template made in step 1, and measure 1cm (½ inch) in and 1cm (½ inch) out from its side and bottom edges, to create a 2.5cm (1 inch) wide frame. Before cutting out the template, extend the lines so that the sides of the frame extend 4cm (1½ inches) beyond the base of the cake, and the base extends 4cm (1½ inches) on either side. Cut out the three-sided template in one piece. Cut 'V' shapes out of each extended end, and cut the tops of the frame at an angle.

11 Make a separate template 2.5cm (1 inch) wide and 12cm (4½ inches) long for the pendulum.

12 Using the template on page 46, make an additional card template for the front roof sections.

13 Roll out some chocolate paste to 2.5mm (⅛ inch) thick and cut out the framework using the template. Gently lift and place on the plastic-covered board. For additional strength, paint the undersides of the pieces that will overhang with a thin layer of melted chocolate. Leave to set.

14 Cut two roof sections for each side, and cut a strip from two of these 1cm (½ inch) in width. Place the roof sections on the plastic-covered board. Use the dresden tool to create a woodgrain effect on all sections.

15 Stick the smaller roof sections on top of the larger using melted chocolate.

16 Using the template made in step 11, cut a strip of paste for the pendulum. Place on the covered board and mark with a woodgrain effect to match the framework.

Decorations

17 Using the templates provided (see page 46), roll and cut out a large bird, adding markings with a dresden tool. Cut two doorways and mark with corn husk. Cut out a door from one of them and stick on top of the whole doorway. Stick the door itself in place. Wrap a thin strip of paste around to complete.

18 Roll out additional paste and cut out six leaves. Place on to a foam pad and vein with the dresden tool. Curl slightly using a ball tool. Cut one extra leaf and vein, but keep flat. This will be used on the pendulum.

19 Model a small ball for the cuckoo's head, mark eyes, and add a beak.

20 Using two 60g (2oz) pieces of chocolate paste, mould two fir cone shapes and snip with a small pair of scissors. Add a small ring at the top of each cone. With bronze powder, dust the cones to give a realistic appearance. Model three tiny nut shapes and snip with scissors.

Assembly

21 Place the clock base on the top portion of the cake board. Using melted chocolate, position and stick the roof to the top of the clock. The roof should overhang the top edge by about 2.5cm (1 inch).

22 Attach the framework, then add the cuckoo doorway, complete with door and cuckoo, above the clock face.

23 Stick the large bird to the apex point and complete the clock with leaves and nuts.

24 Stick the cone weights in position and add chains made from thin crimped strips of chocolate paste. Stick the pendulum to the board as if swinging to the far right. Add the flat leaf.

Celebration Cake

This design illustrates how chocolate paste can be used in the simplest of ways. Frills, flowers, piped lace pieces and a flooded plaque decorate this celebration cake.

Materials

625g (1¼lb) sugarpaste (rolled fondant)
625g (1¼lb) dark chocolate paste
23cm (9 inch) round chocolate cake
Jam and buttercream
Melted chocolate for assembly
90g (3oz) white chocolate chips
60g (2oz) dark chocolate chips
90g (3oz) dark chocolate paste for frills
Gum glue
60g (2oz) white chocolate paste
Selection of petal dusts (blossom tints), including rose and plum
22g (¾oz) green chocolate paste
Cocoa butter

Equipment

30cm (12 inch) round cake board
Sugarpaste smoother
1cm (½ inch) crimper
Nos. 1 and 3 piping tubes (tips)
2 sheets waxed or silicone paper
Medium oval cutter
Scriber
Cocktail sticks (toothpicks)
Plastic sheets
Garrett frill cutter
Thin wooden dowel
Small and medium carnation cutters
Firm foam pad
Ball tool
Craft knife
Dresden tool
Clay gun with discs, optional
Small blossom plunger cutter

Preparing the cake

1 Combine the sugarpaste with 625g (1¼lb) dark chocolate paste to make a chocolate/sugarpaste mix (see page 5). Cut and fill the cake with jam, and mask with butter-cream. Roll out the dark chocolate/sugarpaste mix and use to cover the cake by the all-in-one method (see page 6). Re-knead the scraps of paste into a ball.

2 To coat the board, roll out the remaining paste mix to 2.5mm (⅛ inch) thick. Brush the board with a small amount of sieved jam and lay the paste over it. Use a smoother to iron out any marks in the paste, and trim off excess. Crimp the edge while the paste is still soft. Secure the cake on the board with a little melted chocolate.

3 Melt 60g (2oz) white chocolate chips and add warm water, a drop at a time, stirring after each addition, to thicken slightly. Using a no. 3 tube, pipe a shell border around the base of the cake.

Lace and plaque

4 For the lace pieces, melt the dark chocolate chips and thicken slightly with warm water, as in step 3. Using a no. 1 tube, pipe about 85 lace pieces (see page 47) on to waxed or silicone paper. Allow to set.

5 For the plaque, place a sheet of waxed or silicone paper on a board, and place the oval cutter on the paper. Melt the remaining white chocolate chips and pour into the cutter.

34

Gently lift the board and tap on the work surface to smooth the chocolate and release any air bubbles. Allow to set.

Frills

6 Cut a strip of paper the depth and circumference of the cake and fold into eight equal sections. Cut a scallop from the top, unfold and fit around the cake. Scribe the scallops on to the cake's surface, then remove the template. Push a cocktail stick into each point between the scallops.

7 Roll out the 90g (3oz) dark chocolate paste and cut out eight Garrett frill sections. Using a thin wooden dowel, roll over the edges to frill. Cut the circles to open.

8 Following the scribed scallops on the cake, paint a dropped curved line of glue on the cake side between the markers. Attach the first section of frills, draping it over two cocktail sticks. Continue all the way round the cake. Gently ease the edges of the frills out with a fine dry paintbrush.

9 Roll out 90g (3oz) of the leftover chocolate/sugarpaste mix and repeat steps 7–8 to make a second layer of frills. Remove the sticks.

10 With a small amount of melted chocolate in a piping bag, attach some chocolate lace pieces along the top edge of the frills. Adjust with a dry brush if necessary.

Carnations

11 Roll out the white chocolate paste very thinly. Using the carnation cutters, cut out nine of each size. (Each carnation will need three small and three medium petals.)

16 Gently remove the cocktail sticks and leave the carnations to set for about 1 hour. Dust the edges of the petals with a mixture of rose and plum.

Rope twist

17 Using green chocolate paste, make a 30cm (12 inch) rope twist by hand or with a clay gun fitted with a fine rope disc, and taper each end to a point. Attach to the cake.

Finishing

18 With melted cocoa butter and petal dusts, paint a small picture and a decorative border on the white chocolate oval (see page 47).

19 Attach the oval plaque and flowers to the top of the cake with melted chocolate. Make some small blossoms with a plunger cutter and add to the top of the cake. Attach lace pieces to the edge of the plaque.

12 Transfer to a firm foam pad and gently thin out the cut edges of every petal using a ball tool. Set aside.

13 Place a small petal on the work surface and cut slits into the thinned scalloped edge with a craft knife. Transfer to firm foam and roll over the cut edges with a cocktail stick to frill slightly. Do not press too hard or the edges will stick. Fold in half and concertina (accordion) fold to the centre. Push the blunt end of a cocktail stick into the base and secure.

14 Frill two more small petals, and paint their surfaces with a little gum glue. Attach one to the centre piece by threading the cocktail stick through the centre and gently pressing at the base to secure. Tighten against the centre by pinching tucks in the petal. Repeat for the last small petal.

15 Frill the three medium petals, and attach to the carnation base by painting gum glue on their surfaces and threading the cocktail stick through the centres. Use the pointed end of a dresden tool to open any layers that may have stuck together during assembly. Make two more carnations.

Brush-Embroidered Chocolate Box

This two-in-one cake is the ideal gift, combining a rich fruit cake, decorated to look like a pretty embroidered box, with hand-made sweets.

Materials

750g (1½ lb) dark chocolate paste
Piping gel
Gum glue
Green, red and edible gold petal dusts (blossom tints)
30g (1oz) chocolate chips, melted, for assembly
20cm (8 inch) hexagonal fruit cake covered with marzipan (almond paste)
Vodka
30g (1oz) white chocolate chips
15g (½oz) cocoa butter
Selection of ready-made sweets or candy

Equipment

Plastic sheets
20cm (8 inch) thin hexagonal board covered with gold foil
Plastic doily
Herb cutter
36cm (14 inch) square cake board covered with dark green foil
Ruler
Small rose petal and leaf cutters
Heatproof paint palette

Box lid

1 Roll out 125g (4oz) dark chocolate paste large enough to fit the thin hexagonal board. Emboss the surface with a plastic doily. Paint the reverse side of the hexagonal board with piping gel and attach the paste carefully. Trim to fit.

2 Roll out a long strip of paste and cut with a herb cutter to make several strips 5mm (¼ inch) wide. Paint the board edges with gum glue and gently attach one long strip to create a band edging to the lid.

3 Cut the remaining strips into lengths 13cm (5 inches) long. Cut more to make 40 in all. Pinch the ends of each strip together to form loops. Allow to set on their sides for a few hours. Brush both the loops and the lid edges with edible gold petal dust.

4 To assemble the bow, attach 10 loops in a circle on the lid, laying five on their sides and five flat. Stick in place with melted chocolate. (It might be necessary to trim the ends of the loops to a point to enable you to position them correctly.) Add the remaining loops to create the bow by dipping the ends into melted chocolate and holding in position until the chocolate has set. Place to one side.

Chocolate box

5 Roll out 125g (4oz) chocolate paste 2.5mm (⅛ inch) thick, and large enough to cover the top of the cake. Brush the cake top with vodka. Remove the top sheet of plastic from the paste, and invert the cake on to the paste. Cut around the sides of the cake and remove excess paste. Turn the cake upright and peel off the plastic sheet. Trim the paste if necessary. Place the cake on the square board, placing it towards one corner.

6 Roll out 345g (11oz) paste 2.5mm (⅛ inch) thick. Cut out six panels to fit the sides, adding 2.5cm (1 inch) to the height. Place on a flat surface covered with a plastic sheet.

Brush embroidery

7 Using the drawing on page 47 as a guide, emboss the design into each panel using the rose petal and leaf cutters.

8 Place a heatproof paint palette over boiling water, add a few white chocolate chips to three cups, the cocoa butter to another, and allow to melt. Add a small amount of green petal dust to the chocolate in one, and red petal dust to the other. Gradually mix the dust into the melted chocolate to create depth of colour. Use this to paint the design on to the chocolate panels. To the cocoa butter,

add edible gold dust, and use to paint fine lines on to the design. With a fine brush, touch white centres on to each flower.

Assembly

9 Paint the sides of the cake with vodka and attach each panel carefully, trimming the joins with a craft knife. Roll and cut a strip of paste 2.5cm (1 inch) wide and long enough to fit around the top inside of the box. Attach with gel and trim.

10 Roll out 30g (1oz) chocolate paste thinly and cut six 1cm (½ inch) strips to the height of the cake. Dust each strip with edible gold and attach one to each of the six vertical joins, using a little gum glue. Add a 2.5mm (⅛ inch) strip of chocolate paste to the top of the box rim, to complete the edge.

11 Fill the top of the box with chocolates, arranging them carefully. Lean the lid against the side of the cake.

Autumn Gold Wedding Cake

As chocolate cakes become fashionable, more brides are choosing their cakes for flavour as well as looks. With this American-style two-tier wedding cake, the dark chocolate cake is complemented by the autumn shades of chrysanthemums.

Materials

18cm (7 inch) and 25cm (10 inch) round fruit cakes covered with marzipan (almond paste)
750g (1½lb) white sugarpaste (rolled fondant)
750g (1½lb) dark chocolate paste
Vodka
Gum glue
100g (3½oz) dark chocolate paste for ropes and bows
250g (8oz) white chocolate paste
Selection of paste food colours
Cornflour (cornstarch)

Equipment

36cm (14 inch) thin round cake board covered with bronze foil
Clay gun with discs, optional
Plastic sheets
Small bow cutter
Daisy cutter set 3
Ball tool
Firm and soft foam pads
Chrysanthemum leaf cutter set
Dresden tool

Preparation

1 After covering the cakes with marzipan, leave to stand for 48 hours.

2 Combine the sugarpaste and 750g (1½lb) dark chocolate paste to make a chocolate/sugarpaste mix (see page 5).

3 Brush the marzipan on the cakes with a little vodka. Roll out the dark chocolate/sugarpaste mix and use to cover the two cakes, using the all-in-one method (see page 6). Place the large cake on the cake board. Divide each cake into eight equal sections, marking the top edges with a tiny line.

4 Cut a disc of non-stick paper slightly smaller than the small cake, and place it on top of the large cake, positioning it off centre and towards the back. Place the small cake on the disc. (There is no need to stick the cakes together; the chocolate paste will adhere to itself.)

5 Roll out some more of the paste mix, and cut two strips 5mm (¼ inch) wide to fit around the base of each cake. Fix in position with gum glue.

Rope cords

6 Using a clay gun fitted with a small rope disc, make rope cords with 100g (3½

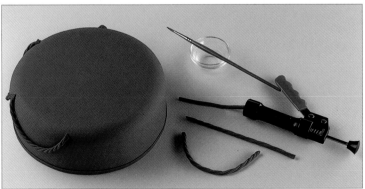

oz) dark chocolate paste. (Roll by hand if you haven't got a clay gun.) Holding one end of the rope in one hand, push your other hand across the paste, creating a twist effect in the rope. Make sixteen 15cm (6 inch) lengths of twisted rope and cover with a sheet of plastic.

7 Brush a tiny amount of gum glue on each of the division markers around the tops of the cakes. Remove one rope section from the plastic, and drape it between two divisions on a cake side, attaching it at each end. Trim the ends. Repeat with the remaining ropes all around the cakes.

Bows

8 Roll out the remaining dark paste and cut out 16 bows. With a little gum glue, attach a bow to every point around the cakes where two draped rope lengths meet.

Chrysanthemums

9 Colour the white chocolate paste in two or three chosen shades, using paste colours. To make the first chrysanthemum, roll some paste to 2.5mm (⅛ inch) thick. Using three graduated sizes of daisy cutter, cut out three large, three medium and two small petals.

10 Lightly dust your hand with cornflour, and place one of the large petals in your palm. With a ball tool, gently draw each petal from the centre out to the tip to lengthen and widen. Keep the petal moving all the time to make sure the paste does not stick to your hand. Transfer the petal to a firm foam pad and, with the small end of the ball tool, draw each petal from the tip in towards the centre to cup the ends. Place the petal on a work surface that has been lightly dusted with cornflour.

11 Repeat step 10 for the remaining two large petals. Glue the centre of the first petal and place the second petal on top, turning the flower to stagger the petals. Gently push with the large end of the ball tool to fix. Add the third large petal in the same way. Repeat the process with the medium and small petals, but as you get smaller in petal size, cup the ends more, to create a tighter array of petals, so that the centre of the flower does not show. Repeat to make as many chrysanthemums as you require.

Leaves

12 Roll out some green paste and cut a selection of different-sized leaves. Place on a firm foam pad. Using a dresden tool, mark veins on the leaves and, with the large end of the ball tool, thin the edges slightly. Place on a soft foam pad to shape, and leave to dry.

Assembly

13 Create the shape of the sprays first on a board, positioning the leaves and flowers. To angle the large flower heads, place a wedge of chocolate paste beneath.

14 Transfer the flower sprays to the cakes, attaching the leaves first with a little gum glue, and then adding the flowers carefully, also attaching with gum glue.

Fruit Barrel

This chocolate paste fruit barrel makes an attractive and unusual cake, suitable for a man's birthday or other celebration.

Materials

Two 15cm (6 inch) round madeira cakes, each 7.5cm (3 inches) high
Jam and buttercream
345g (11oz) dark chocolate paste
60g (2oz) black chocolate paste
Piping gel
Selection of hand-made marzipan (almond paste) fruits (apples, pears, cherries and grapes), and leaves

Equipment

Sharp serrated knife
30cm (12 inch) oval cake board covered with green foil
Plastic sheets
Round cutter
Corn husk
Large plain writing tube (tip)

Shaping cake

1 Cut and layer both cakes with jam, and stack together using buttercream. Using a sharp serrated knife, taper the top and bottom, trimming at an angle all the way round, to create a barrel shape.

2 Mask the top and sides with buttercream, and place on the cake board.

Covering

3 Roll out enough dark paste to cover the top of the barrel, and use a round cutter to cut out a disc of paste to fit the top. Place a round piece of plastic on top of this to prevent fingerprints when attaching the side panels.

4 Roll out 315g (10oz) dark paste fairly thinly in a wide strip slightly wider than the depth of the cake. Using a long piece of corn husk, emboss the entire strip to give a woodgrain effect.

5 Cut the paste into strips slightly longer than the height of the barrel and approximately 5cm (2 inches) wide. Taper each strip by cutting a small amount from each corner.

6 Attach a panel to the cake, starting at the bottom and gently pressing the panel against the cake until you reach the top, making sure that the panel is slightly higher than the top of the cake. Continue attaching the remaining panels.

7 Roll the black paste into a long thin strip. Cut out two bands, each 1cm (½ inch) wide. Place one band around the barrel a third of the way down, and the other a third of the way up. Secure the bands with a small amount of piping gel. Mark rivets in these bands, two per panel, using the tip of a plain round writing tube.

Cork

8 Make the barrel cork by cutting out a brown disc with the other end of the writing tube. Give it a woodgrain effect with the husk and position it on the barrel side. Secure with piping gel.

Fruit

9 Position the marzipan fruits in the barrel, starting with the grapes hanging down on each side of the barrel. Fill in with the other fruits and leaves. Place extra fruits on the board.

Templates

Cuckoo Clock
(page 30)
Cuckoo's doorway

Cuckoo Clock
(page 30)
clock hands

Cuckoo Clock
(page 30)
bird decoration

Cuckoo Clock
(page 30)
roof front